my DOG IS BLIND
– but lives life to the full!

The guide to every aspect of a happy life with
a blind or sight-impaired dog

Hubble & Hattie

For more than eighteen years, the folk at Veloce have concentrated their publishing efforts on all-things automotive. Now, in a break with tradition, the company launches a new imprint for a new publishing genre!
The Hubble & Hattie imprint – so-called in memory of two, dearly-loved West Highland Terriers – will be the home of a range of books that cover all things animal, all produced to the same high quality of content and presentation as our motoring books, and offering the same great value for money.

For Elliott
And for Hubble and Hattie

Translated by Anna McLuckie

Photo credits:
Pages 8, 9, 11, 13, 22, 23, 30, 32, 40, 55, 56, 60, 64, 68, 73: bottom left; middle right, 74: top right; middle left; bottom right: Jude Brooks
Page 39: Dietmar Steuernagel
Pages 52 & 73: Susanne Erdelji
Pages 69, 74: bottom left: Niki Renshaw
Page 74: Katharina Niederhauser
All other photos: Nicole Horsky

www.hubbleandhattie.com

First published in English in February 2010 by Veloce Publishing Limited, Veloce House, Parkway Farm Business Park, Poundbury, Dorchester DT1 3AR, England.
Fax 01305 250479/e-mail: info@hubbleandhattie.com/web: www.hubbleandhattie.com.
ISBN: 978-1-845842-91-8 UPC: 6-36847-04291-2
Original publication © 2009 Kynos Verlag, Dr Dieter Fleig GmbH. www.kynos-verlag.de
Readers with ideas for books about animals, or animal-related topics, are invited to write to the editorial director of Veloce Publishing at the above address.
British Library Cataloguing in Publication Data – A catalogue record for this book is available from the British Library. Typesetting, design and page make-up all by Veloce Publishing Ltd on Apple Mac. Printed in India by Imprint Digital.

Contents

Introduction

Elliott is six years old, a pointer cross who looks like a bear. He's often called 'Cuddle monster,' because he can snuggle up to you for hours! He is always in a good mood, always ready to play, and the greatest home help you could wish for: he can turn lights on and off, roll up carpets and open kitchen cupboards. At the moment he is learning to sort the laundry.

At home, he generally spends his time lying on the sofa with his legs stretched out. When you stop stroking him, he grunts and prods you with a paw.

Elliot's favourite game is hide and seek. He knows the names of his toys and likes learning new tricks. When I ask him what 1 and 1 makes, he barks twice. Sometimes he miscalculates and then 1 and 1 makes eight!

Elliott is a very sociable dog. He very much loves the people he knows and likes to spend all day with them. Strangers frighten him, but that's okay; I have learnt how to deal with it, and he has learnt that they are okay if I say they are. When I notice that he is feeling very uneasy, we just take a turn around the block.

Elliott loves being taken out in the car. Even if it's a long drive, he looks out of the window, has a bit of a sleep, and then looks out of the window some more.

What exactly Elliott sees, I will probably never know, as Elliott is almost blind. He has some residual vision but can perceive only light/dark contrasts. He has too few optic nerves: information that is taken in by the lens can't be sent to his brain.

Elliott was about ten weeks old when he came to live with me. When I saw him for the first time, I knew that unless I took him, no one was going to. He sat in the corner and would not let anyone touch him. I took him home.

He took the standard, speedy path of a modern city dog: puppy training classes, companion dog test, trailing and agility. He was the best in every group and came in the top three in every competition: the fact that he sometimes collided with obstacles didn't worry anyone. They told me it was normal. And just bad luck that he always had an upset stomach.

Elliott was always nervous, staying glued to my side and giving the impression that he thought the sky might fall on his head at any moment. He barked at people when they wanted to touch him and ran in a circle all the time. He was suffering and crying out for help, but for a whole year I couldn't hear him.

When he was one-and-a-half years old, I understood at last that this was not a happy dog and began to look for help. Along the way, I met many dog trainers – some were good, some not so good – but none was able to help Elliott, wanting only to treat the symptoms rather than find the cause of his behaviour.

By this stage, Elliott was displaying severe behavioural problems. He was frightened of life, could no longer walk past strangers, and lived in a constant state of readiness to defend himself; he was sick with fear.

I finally found a trainer who recognised that his problems might have an organic cause. She sent us to a veterinary clinic where Elliott was diagnosed as blind. I went through every conceivable emotion: anger, guilt, sympathy. How could I have lived with a creature for one-and-a-half years and not notice what was wrong with him?

Thankfully, Elliott has since developed into a happy dog, who greets every day with a smile. He is just like any other canine apart from the fact that he has only four senses.

On our journey, I have met lots of amazing people with fascinating blind dogs, owners who give so much in terms of warmth and affection, and

are so patient with all those who ask why they didn't just have their dog put to sleep. They are one reason that I am happy to have written this book, which aims to demonstrate that blind dogs can live very well with their disability, and can do almost everything that sighted dogs can. I hope that my book will support you and bolster your confidence for making the most of life with your companion, regardless of whether he or she was blind from birth, or has gone blind as a result of ageing or illness.

Chapter 1

Diagnosed as blind – what now?

How will you deal with it?

When I found out that my dog was blind, at first, I was simply bewildered – and then I felt guilty and sad. I was also angry as it seemed so unjust, and laid the blame on anyone who happened to be around. Fundamentally, I was powerless, and it was probably this that caused me to feel fearful about how to cope with my dog.

These kinds of feelings are common when people are confronted with the fact that their dog is going blind. If the blindness is sudden, you are thrown into the situation and have to adapt as quickly as possible. If your dog goes blind more gradually, you have some time to adjust to the new situation and come to terms with it.

Blindness with no prospect of a cure means that it is up to the owner to make the adjustments and changes, and regard it as an opportunity. We call our domestic dogs 'man's best friend,' and this is our chance to be a best friend to

our dog, and support him or her in their hour of need.

It is normal and important to be sad, because only then can we learn how to deal with the situation. Many owners are bewildered, as I was; some are shocked and immediately think that the only course of action is to have their pet put to sleep; others simply take everything as it comes.

If you belong to the first group, it is important to be aware that your animal will have less of a problem with his loss of sight than would you. One sense will be lost, yes, but this will serve to sharpen the others; as it is, with up to 100 times as many olfactory receptors as a human, a dog really 'sees' with his nose, anyway! He will have to adapt to his new circumstances, but he will make the best of it.

You may not be able to face facts immediately after the diagnosis; you may, perhaps, not want to believe it, and will seek a second and even a third opinion, and it's

right that you should do this. Vets are human, too, and, as such, can make mistakes, so don't shy away from consulting several vets as this will also help you come to terms with the situation and slowly get to grips with it, and the reality of it. It is important that veterinary staff also take care of the dog owner, clarify issues, and reduce his or her anxiety.

It is a fact that blind dogs can live wonderful lives: they can run across fields, catch balls, relax in the sun, or stare out of the window for hours. And you needn't feel isolated – even if you do at first – because you don't know anyone else with a blind dog, or have considered whether or not there may exist contented dogs which cannot see. You may not be shown much understanding in your immediate environment post-diagnosis, which can increase your feelings of isolation, and it's okay to cry and

express your pain because of this, though I do think it's important not to burden your dog with this unnecessarily. The human has to be there for the dog in this case, and not the other way around.

The final phase in the process is acceptance, following which, you will come to understand that a blind dog is really not very different to a sighted one.

The phases that you may go through demonstrate that you are normal. You don't have to suppress any of them – it is human to be

Although blind, Hubble was always very interested in what was going on!

angry and sad, because loss causes sadness – but you must not forget that this is not about you; it is about your dog – a living being with feelings and fears, strengths and weaknesses. Be there for your best friend.

How will your dog deal with it?

Just like humans, dogs are individuals with unique characters, and, because of this, each will cope differently with blindness.

A dog that has been blind from birth doesn't know any different, and so doesn't miss what he's never had; dogs that *go* blind, however, have first to get used to their new situation. Some will need longer than others to do this, but sooner or later all of them will achieve this, provided they can rely on their owner to become their 'guide person.'

Loss of sight, blindness and visual impairment have a variety of causes, are analysed on an individual basis, and experienced and managed in different ways. It is possible that some dogs may exhibit depressive behaviour initially, whereas others may suffer from nervous aggression; some scarcely change at all. Your dog's reaction depends on certain factors:

- How old is your dog?
- Is he healthy and therefore able to adapt quickly to this new state, or does he have infirmities that could make it harder to adjust? For instance, is he deaf?
- How was his basic compliance before loss of sight occurred: did he come reliably when called? A dog who was not compliant before he went blind is obviously not going to behave any better once he is blind!
- What type of personality does he have, and how is his relationship with people? Is your dog shy or self-confident, independent-minded or timid?
- Are there any other dogs in the immediate environment from whom he could get his bearings?
- How much time does the owner have for the pet that is losing his sight?

Fear and aggression

Many dogs react to blindness with fear and aggression. Put yourself in your dog's place: he can no longer see, and, initially, has no way of assessing danger. Sometimes he may be frustrated and angry because he has not yet memorised his environment and where everything is; he may still bump into a chair, and have to shake himself and carry on. From time to time he will perhaps be bad-tempered and over-wrought, because this new situation is very tiring for him, so he may react by growling because he is frightened and can't get his bearings. This is all completely normal and to be expected.

To help with this have areas in your home where your dog can be completely relaxed and peaceful, but still with you, to reassure him and soothe his anxiety.

Observe your dog. Where is his favourite spot to lie? It is important to really leave the dog in peace, if that's what he wants, and ensure that all family members do likewise.

If your dog should growl on occasion when you approach, do not scold him, as he is only trying to tell you in his way that he doesn't feel good and doesn't want you to come any closer. Before this happens, it is likely he will exhibit behaviour that shows how he is feeling, so study your dog in order to help him where appropriate.

Depression
Dogs can suffer from depression in the same way that people can, and this may be expressed by a decrease in activity and loss of interest in pursuits that he enjoyed before losing his sight, such as playing or going for a walk.

If you feel that your dog is depressed, consider whether he could be this way because of how you are feeling. Our dogs are the mirrors of our soul, so maybe you are projecting your feelings onto him. Take care and try to ensure that your dog is shielded from your mood if this is the case.

Dependence
Some dogs can lapse into total dependence on you, no longer able to walk without their human by their side, which demonstrates a lack of self-confidence. Whether he was already lacking in self-confidence before losing his sight, or whether it declined after he went blind is of significance, but, in both cases, sensitive handling is needed to enable him to develop more self-assurance. This book will give you ideas for games and exercises that will help you achieve this objective.

Hattie was always very independent.

See page 12 for more about Hubble and Hattie

Chapter 2

The question of euthanasia

I have heard it said that it would be better to have a blind dog put to sleep. This statement is usually made by people who don't have a blind dog themselves, have never seen one, and can't imagine themselves continuing to live if they lost *their* sense of sight.

I have heard it said that it would be better to have a blind dog put to sleep because – allegedly – her quality of life will be less than that of a sighted dog. Of course, this is not true; quality of life does not depend on what a dog can see or hear but on completely different things, such as how she is treated and what sort of life she has. Moreover, a dog that is born blind cannot miss what she has never known, and a dog that goes blind has to first come to terms with this new state, which can be accomplished quite easily with your help.

I have heard it said that it would be better to have a blind dog put to sleep because she will be in constant pain from bumping into things. This is complete rubbish. Of course, it's possible that she may occasionally bump into something, but this is only likely in new and unknown environments, and not in her usual, familiar habitats. Additionally, you can be your dog's eyes and responsible for guiding her: when she receives the correct guidance, very rarely will she will bump into objects.

I have heard it said that it would be better to put a blind dog to sleep because she won't be able to mix with other dogs, as she will be unable to see and read their body language. It is true to say that your dog won't be able to read the body language of other canines, but this doesn't mean that she will be cantankerous with dogs she meets. Your dog can learn rituals and signal words that will help her to understand what she can expect in a particular situation; for instance, that she is now about to meet another dog. How to go about this is detailed later in this book.

I have heard it said that a blind dog is untrainable and uncontrollable, and can never be let off the lead. Of course, this is not true either. My blind dog, Elliott, is rather more obedient than many dogs, which may be because he is strongly focused on me. Aside from that, his other senses are accentuated. Blind dogs know exactly who is where! Blind dogs can walk off-lead, you just have to guide them correctly and warn them if there is an obstacle in their path. In town, no dog should be off-lead anyway, because of the risk that they may run across the road.

Loss of sight is never a reason to have a dog put to sleep, or to isolate her or subject her to other mental or physical harm. It is necessary to carry out some research and advisable to have access to competent trainers, who know what to do when a blind dog comes to them for training, and it is not correct to say that a blind dog makes exactly the same demands of its owner as does a sighted dog.

You have to work differently with her and guide her appropriately through her environment. Remember, even training a sighted dog is not always easy!

It may be the case that you will not get a great deal of support and understanding from the people around you. Consider carefully how you will deal with this, and especially how you will react.

Case history
HUBBLE & HATTIE

West Highland White sisters Hubble and Hattie were fairly typical of their breed in that they suffered the usual skin problems. Additionally, both developed keratoconjunctivitus (dry eye) when they were about 10 years old, followed by diabetes and then blindness (first Hubble, then Hattie).

Hubble's blindness occurred practically overnight (though she had had dry eye for some while by then) when she went with Hattie, new dog Immie, and their owner, Jude, to live in Northern Cyprus. She had just a matter of weeks before been diagnosed as diabetic, and it could be that the stress of the flight and change in her environment precipitated her blindness. Whatever the reason, it was a frightening and confusing time for Hubble but, in her usual stoical way, she coped very well with it, although losing her sight did dent her confidence, resulting in her withdrawing somewhat, and becoming less responsive to stimuli that was new or foreign to her. A cataract removal operation was carried out on her left eye whilst in Cyprus, but this was not successful.

During her time in Cyprus, Hubble gradually became unhappy about walking on a lead, which made walks rather problematic until Jude hit on the idea of carrying her in a rucksack on her back, stopping halfway for Hubble to have a 'toilet break' and a sniff around! Once back in the UK, this mode of transport was joined by a petmobile, which Hubble absolutely loved riding in, and which generated much comment when Jude and the dogs were out and about!

Some time after returning to the UK, Hattie developed diabetes and it soon became obvious that her eyesight was failing. Another cataract removal operation was carried out which seemed, at first, hopeful. Sadly, it was not successful and Hattie lost what little sight she had left.

Life with two blind dogs was interesting, to say the least, especially as both Westies required twice-daily insulin injections to control their diabetes. At times, it was hard going, though always worthwhile, as both girls still obviously enjoyed their lives very much, pottering in the garden, laying in the sun, or tucking into their food. They were never a problem to take out, and always went on holiday with Jude and her then partner ; to France, several times, Scotland, and even on a narrowboat! (In fact, during this holiday, Hubble calmly walked off the towpath and into the canal, from which she had to be fished out with a boat hook: she took it all in her stride!) They were sometimes an irritation to Immie as quite often they would walk into her, or tread on her when she was lying down; Immie would growl to warn them and this would make Hubble and Hattie anxious about moving sometimes. Despite this, they both found their way around remarkably well, even going up and down stairs without hesitation.

The average life expectancy of a dog once she develops diabetes is 15 months, but both Hubble and Hattie lived until they were 14; some four years after diagnosis. Living with her two blind dogs is something that Jude is glad she has experienced, and it certainly wouldn't put her off doing so again, although she stresses that it does require a certain level of commitment.

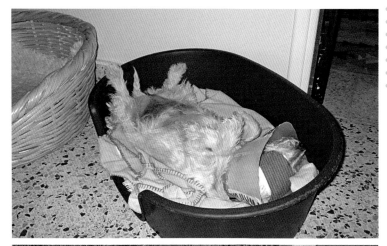

Hubble, rather relaxed – and sporting jaunty red bandage – not long after her cataract operation.

Hubble never missed out on walks – even if she didn't do a lot of walking!

In her petmobile, Hubble would sometimes actually fall asleep!

Chapter 3

The sense of sight

I believe there are six senses: touch, taste, smell, sight, hearing, and balance. In principle, and in the broadest terms, the system and structure of the sense organs are the same across the animal kingdom; the differences are in the performance and use of the senses, and in the perceptions engendered by the adaptation of individual species to its environment. So, for example, humans rely more on their sense of sight, whilst dogs are more dependent on their sense of smell.

The dog's olfactory area is approximately 15 times larger than a human's, and houses 220 million receptor cells (a human has aound 5 million). However, a dog doesn't utilise all of this immense capability. When searching for food in the wild, it is important that the animal receives the maximum amount of nutrition for the minimum amount of expended energy. Therefore, a dog will use his eyes, ears and nose to search for food, and, although the olfactory sense is the strongest, he employs his eyes first, then his ears, and lastly his nose, because using his nose is very strenuous in terms of energy. A sighted dog will always try to deal with what comes his way by first using his eyes.

The eye

Light beams travel through the pupil and the lens to reach the light-sensitive receptors at the back of the eye, which stimulate the nerves to send signals to the brain. The lens focuses the light beams and provides a clear image of the viewed object on the retina at the back of the eye. The retina is composed of light-sensitive receptors and thin nerve cells which transfer the luminous impression to the brain. The photoreceptors react to the light and send signals via the thin nerve fibres to the optic nerve, which lead from the back of the eye to the brain.

How a sighted dog sees the world

Previously, it was assumed that dogs

Structure of the eye

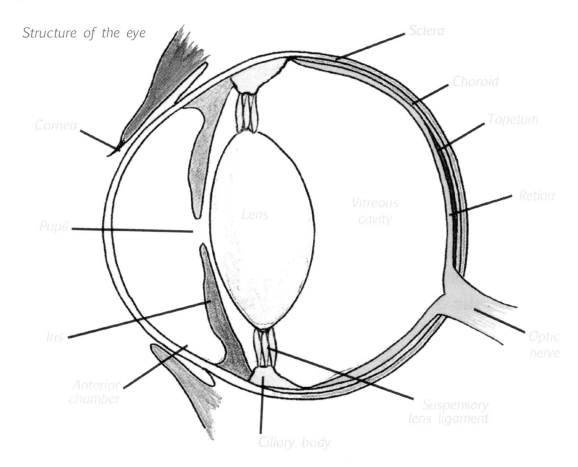

Sclera

Choroid

Tapetum

Cornea

Retina

Vitreous cavity

Lens

Pupil

Iris

Optic nerve

Anterior chamber

Suspensory lens ligament

Ciliary body

were colour-blind and could see in black and white only. Now, however, we know that this is not the case, and that dogs can very probably distinguish colours, though they do have red/green colour blindness.

Every creature has developed the visual system that is best suited to help it survive. Before the dog was domesticated, he hunted for prey early in the morning and at twilight, so his eyes are best suited to these times of day. The retina of the eye contains rods and retinal cones. Rods distinguish light and dark, but are very photosensitive. Retinal cones, on the other hand,

assist with vision in medium to bright light conditions, and with perceiving colour. Dogs have a particularly large number of rods in the retina, whilst the human eye has about five times as many retinal cones. The modest number of rods in the canine retina leads to the conclusion that this is an eye specialised in the area of photosensitivity rather than colour perception.

Human visual acuity is about six times better than that of dogs. Dogs can barely recognise still objects from a distance, but can certainly detect the slightest movement from far away.

Visual acuity is influenced by the size of the pupil, the lens and the cornea, and by the configuration of rods and retinal cones. The size of the pupil changes depending on the intensity of light exposure. When light is poor, dogs have an advantage over humans, because their pupils are bigger than humans', which gives better sight in poor light conditions. However, the rod system does not enable good visual acuity, although a light-reflecting film at the back of the dog's eye – the tapetum lucidum – enables the dog to perceive shapes and movement. Canine sight is particularly specialised in discerning movement in poor light conditions, as this is essential to survival as a hunter in the wild.

Another anatomical speciality which is helpful when hunting is the dog's wide range of vision which, depending on breed, can be anything from 240 to 270 degrees, compared to the 200 degree range of vision of humans. However, the area that is seen by both eyes (the binocular range of vision) is smaller, but is important for spatial depth perception (stereo vision), and in this area human sight is stronger than that of the dog.

We humans see far more colour and detail than do our dogs, but this does not mean that the dog is disadvantaged. The dog, like all animals, developed sight that best assists his survival in the wild.

Sight loss

Blindness in this context is taken to mean vision of a maximum of two per cent, or 1/50; anything above this is described as severely impaired sight. The way that your dog loses his sight has a strong bearing on how he will cope with it. Dogs which are blind from birth do not know any different and generally cope very well: after all, you can't miss what you've never had.

Animals which lose their sight suddenly have it the hardest, as they have no time to adjust. Some illnesses can cause sight loss to occur quite quickly, and in this case, you can expect your dog to suffer from severe confusion, at least initially.

When the loss of sight is gradual, the implication is that the animal will at least be able to slowly acclimatise to his change in visual capability.

Fleeting blindness means that the dog will lose his sight for a certain period, which can be very confusing, and some dogs may not regain full sight. When a dog is very stressed (by surroundings or living circumstances, etc), it may be the case that he will see less well than he is actually organically capable of doing. Should this happen, it is important that the dog has the opportunity of finding some peace and quiet so that his eyes can recover.

Some dogs are night-blind and cannot see in certain lighting conditions; this affects more dogs than is commonly supposed.

Blindness can also occur as part of the ageing process, when cataracts develop.

Chapter 4

Eye examination and symptoms

Many dog owners have little background knowledge about their dog's state of health. They can often not determine exactly what is wrong with their companion, and are stressed and confused as a result. They trust the vet and place the fate of their dog in her hands, without making inquiries or carrying out any research or investigation. It is completely normal to be stunned after receiving a particularly serious and life-changing diagnosis, and not really able to take in what the medical professional is saying; in fact, psychologists have determined that patients generally forget 80 per cent of what they are told in the doctor's surgery!

It is important to put aside your inhibitions and ask questions, and, if not sure about something, get another opinion. Follow your gut instinct and you probably won't go wrong. Don't be afraid of going back to the vet several times, and insist that they make time for you. Write down any questions that occur to you at home and take them with you next time you visit. Don't be afraid to write down what the vet tells you, and don't rest until you are sure you have understood everything.

Eye examination

Although dogs are primarily dependent on their sense of smell, their sense of sight, as discussed previously, is still extremely important.

When sight is lost, it means that there is only limited communication with the environment, and so eye condition should therefore be checked during every routine examination. Early diagnosis and prevention are the most important issues here! Many eye diseases are only presented to the vet once irreversible damage has already occurred, so an eye examination should be an integral part of any clinical examination.

Ensure that your vet examines your dog thoroughly and completely, and checks the condition of her eyes at the beginning of the consultation.

If there is any indication that your dog's vision has worsened, the vet should test her sight at the beginning of the examination. When a dog is under stress, her vision deteriorates, as explained earlier, and most dogs experience a great deal of stress when visiting the vet.

It is not possible to use subjective sight tests, of course, so the few objective investigative tests which determine the degree of sight must be carefully carried out. It is easier to measure a human's range of vision, as they can say what and how much they see.

In a healthy canine eye, the pupil contracts when it is exposed to light, so that the components in the area at the back of the eye (lens, retina and vitreous body) can no longer by properly evaluated. It is for this reason that the dog will be given eye drops (Mydricaine, for example) to expand the pupil, and these will take effect after about 10 or 20 minutes.

The initial eye examination will involve using light to gauge the size of the pupils, and reaction to light will be tested in both eyes in order to prevent the pupil reflex which occurs through repeated exposure to light. One eye will then be examined in detail. In principle, the healthy-looking eye (if there is one) should be examined first. Examination of the interior of the eye, the second examination, takes place in a darkened room, so that the vet will not be distracted by the eye's reflex reactions to light.

Examination methods

• OPHTHALMOSCOPY

An ophthalmoscopy is an examination of the area at the back of the eye, during which the examiner can observe the internal surface of the eyeball. Using magnifying lenses and light sources, the examiner looks through the pupil into the inside of the eye.

There are both direct and indirect ophthalmoscopies: in a direct ophthalmoscopy the ophthalmoscope is positioned very close to the patient's eye, and the vet looks directly into the eye using 16x magnification. However, this enables the vet to see only a small segment of the eye. In an indirect ophthalmoscopy, the back of the eye is examined from a distance of about 50cm using a light source. During the examination, a magnifying lens is held 2-10cm in front of the dog's eye.

• SLIT LAMP EXAMINATION (BIOMICROSCOPY)

A slit lamp examination is the microscopic examination of the transparent structure of the eye (cornea, anterior chamber, lens and eye ball), which can also detect clouding and deposits. A microscope with a slit lamp attached is used for this examination. The lamp emits a narrow slice of light that enables an optical examination of the transparent sections of the ocular tissue.

• TONOMETRY

Tonometry measures the intra-ocular pressure, as, for instance, in the case of glaucoma. In addition, it detects inflammation inside the eye. Normal intra-ocular pressure is generally 10-23mmHg.

SONOGRAPHY
A sonography is an examination of the eye using ultrasound. The surface of the eye is numbed with eye drops and an ultrasound probe is placed directly on the eye. The images produced are then visible on a screen.

In addition, your dog may undergo the following tests:

OBSTACLE COURSE
With one eye covered your dog is led through a room containing stationary obstacles (a broom handle positioned slightly above floor level, for instance); the exercise is then repeated with the other eye covered. Alternatively, your dog may be let off the lead and called by you from the other side of the obstacles. I would advise against using the latter test, however, as I regard it as a betrayal of trust: imagine how your dog might feel if you were to call her to you and, just before she gets to you, she stumbles over an obstacle.

In order to gauge how a dog deals with obstacles, it should be sufficient to carefully observe her in a room in which she has never before been. Look out for your dog taking far bigger steps over an obstacle than is necessary.

COTTON WOOL TEST
A fairly small ball of cotton wool is dropped in front of the dog. The sighted dog's gaze will follow the slowly falling ball of cotton wool (silent, odourless, no air movement), if she has never experienced either the cotton wool or the test process before. Most dogs will become increasingly uninterested if the test is repeated, however.

OPTICAL TABLE EDGE TEST
If you lift your dog and move towards the edge of a table as if to place her on it, she will try to put her front or back paw on the table. (I have my reservations about this test, particularly if the dog has learnt previously that she is going to be put on something as soon as she is lifted up, as she will be expecting this and react accordingly.)

MENACE REFLEX
The menace reflex is exhibited when a hand movement is made towards the eye – the eyelid closes and the head may move to the side. It usually only has limited clinical diagnostic relevance, however.

Common diseases
Some diseases are associated with sight loss. Please note that the following list is in no way comprehensive, although it will provide an overview. It should also not take the place of a visit to your vet.

PRA (PROGRESSIVE RETINAL ATROPHY)
Progressive retinal atrophy is the gradual death of the retina. There are two types: an early onset variant, where blindness occurs by the age of 12 months, and a late onset variant, where the first problems with vision appear between the ages of three and six years. The second variant is the most common

and is a recessively inherited disorder, which means that dogs with PRA can have healthy parents and siblings; the parents are simply genetic carriers in this case.

In the early stages of the disease, the owner notices that the dog's pupils are larger and remarkably luminous at night, at which point the dog is generally already exhibiting some significant degree of night-blindness. Dogs so afflicted will often refuse to go outside at twilight or at night, or will bump into objects that they can still see during the day. The night-blindness will become noticeably worse and the daytime vision increasingly impaired until the dog finally goes completely blind.

This progressive retinal degeneration is not painful, and the dog has enough time to get used to her disability. Often, dogs affected by this disease compensate so successfully that it only first becomes noticeable when they find themselves in an unfamiliar environment.

There is no treatment and no way to influence the course of the disease. Breeds which are particularly susceptible to this condition are miniature poodles, English cocker spaniels and labradors. The disease develops in these breeds after they reach reproductive maturity.

- ### RPED (RETINAL PIGMENT EPITHELIAL DYSTROPHY)
RPED was previously known as central progressive retinal atrophy (CPRA), and was renamed for aetiological and clinical reasons.

Stationary objects are recognised less well than moving ones (loss of central vision). The loss of sight takes place gradually, and sometimes occurs in older animals. Treatment is limited to alleviating painful conditions associated with the disease, such as glaucoma.

Breeds particularly commonly affected with this problem are labradors and golden retrievers, English cocker and springer spaniels, Welsh corgi, border collies, collies, shelties, and briards.

- ### RETINAL DYSPLASIA (RD)
RD is a polymorphic disease, characterised by folding of the retina. It is hereditary. The disease is difficult to identify, as the symptoms are clinically inconspicuous. The folds on the retina are white in appearance. The breeds affected by this condition include collies, American cocker spaniels, beagles, labradors, rottweilers, Yorkshire terriers, cavalier King Charles spaniels, English springer spaniels, and German shepherds.

- ### NEURORETINITIS (SARD)
Neuroretinitis is a disease of the retina that generally affects both eyes. It causes a sudden loss of sight and can occur as the result of an infection, such as distemper. Usually, however, it is an abnormal immunoreaction without an identifiable cause.

SARD stands for sudden acquired retinal degeneration. The onset of blindness can occur within one day or a few weeks, and is particularly prevalent among dachshunds.

- ### GLAUCOMA
The term glaucoma is used to

describe a morbid increase in intra-ocular pressure – normal intra-ocular pressure in dogs is 10-23mmHg – which occurs when the acqueous humour (fluid in the eye) does not drain properly. This often causes severe pain and damages the eye, specifically the cells of the retina and the optic nerve. The pressure is measured under local anaesthetic (eye drops) with a tonometer. Glaucoma is one of the most frequent causes of blindness in dogs.

The disease can occur spontaneously (primary glaucoma), or develop as a consequence of another eye disease (secondary glaucoma). Breeds genetically predisposed to this condition include the American cocker spaniel, basset hound, bouvier des Flandres, Entlebucher mountain dog, flat coated retriever, and Siberian husky.

The condition is treated initially with drugs which reduce intra-ocular pressure and relieve the pain. If there is no success over the longer term with this treatment, an operation may be necessary, depending on the primary cause of the glaucoma. The chances of successfully saving the dog's sight depend on the cause of the glaucoma and on starting treatment early. Important note: your dog should immediately start wearing a chest harness instead of a collar as pulling on the collar is known to increase intra-ocular pressure.

● CATARACT
A common clause of blindness in dogs, a cataract is a clouding of the lens that either affects the entire lens or individual sections of it. The lens causes a refraction and brings objects into focus on the retina. If the lens is severely clouded, the retina is no longer exposed to light and the animal goes blind. Cataracts arise from genetic defects, as a result of aging, or as a consequence of inflammation, tumours, diabetes, or diseases of the retina. Breeds most frequently affected by this condition include the poodle, cocker spaniel, Yorkshire terrier, beagle, small Münsterlander and West Highland white terrier.

It is possible to surgically remove the lens. An incision of approximately 5cm is made in the cornea, the lens broken up using ultrasound and extracted. Cataract operations are not always successful, however, as the longer the cataract has been in existence, the greater the likelihood of complications.

● KERATOCONJUNCTIVITIS SICCA (KCS) OR 'DRY EYE'
KCS is the consequence of a disease of the tear ducts associated with diminished tear production. The tear film becomes deficient and the cornea begins to dry out. If the disease is left untreated it can lead to blindness, or even loss of the eye.

KCS can be diagnosed by means of a quick and simple test (the Schirmer tear test) which measures tear production.

Breeds which have a predisposition for this condition include the West Highland white terrier, bulldog, cocker spaniel, beagle, Yorkshire terrier and lhasa apso. The disease is seen more often in female and elderly animals.

Winnie has cataracts in both eyes.

Initial treatment is with drugs – symptoms can be alleviated by the use of lubricating drops such as Viscotears™ – and an operation may be recommended in individual cases.

● GERMAN SHEPHERD KERATITIS (PANNUS OR CHRONIC SUPERFICIAL KERATITIS)
German shepherd keratitis is a disease of the cornea. As indicated by the name, it frequently affects

See page 68 for more about Winnie

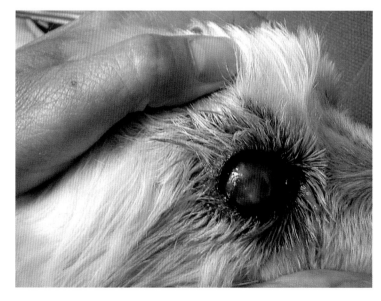

Hattie shortly after her cataract operation. Blood vessels formed across her eye and obscured her vision.

German shepherds and German shepherd crosses.

The cornea is the external section of the eye. In its healthy state, it is transparent, 0.5-1mm thick, and consists of four different layers. The term keratitis includes corneal inflammations which occur as a consequence of injuries or irritation resulting in inflammation, either on the interior or exterior of the eyeball. These include any accumulation of fluid in the cornea, the

Diminished tear production results in a thick, mucus-like substance, which dries and crusts around the eye.

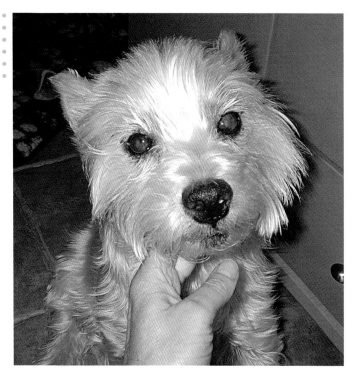

growth of blood vessels into the cornea, which normally has no vessels, and occurrence of pigmentation deposits.

In German shepherd keratitis, blood vessels and pigment deposits appear in the cornea. The first symptoms are red and white or shiny deposits on the outer edge of the cornea, which then spread. It is assumed that this disease is an allergic reaction with an unknown cause, which attacks the body's own tissue; ie an auto-immune disorder.

The disease proceeds in phases and usually affects both eyes, generally first appearing between the ages of three and five years and eventually leading to the complete loss of sight. In order to prevent or weaken the effect of further phases of the disease, affected dogs must wear goggles with UV protection, as direct exposure to sunlight results in more acute attacks.

IRITIS AND UVEITIS

Beneath the external surface of the eyeball is the uvea, a layer well-supplied with blood vessels. Inflammation of the iris (responsible for eye colour) and the uvea is a very dangerous disease and must be dealt with quickly to prevent lasting damage. These inflammations can have various causes, for example: external trauma; inflammation in the area around the eye or elsewhere in the body, infestation of parasites, infections, metabolic disorders or poisoning.

CEA (COLLIE EYE ANOMALY)

This hereditary disease primarily affects collies and shelties, but is also increasingly found in related breeds such as Australian shepherds and border collies. It is an anomaly of the retina that can affect dogs to varying degrees. Vision is only slightly impaired with some dogs, whilst others can suffer a detached retina or a haemorrhage in the eye, which can lead to blindness. CEA does worsen over time.

Puppies of breeds at risk of this

condition should undergo specialist tests at the age of 6-8 weeks to detect the presence or otherwise of the anomaly. Animals with this condition may not be used for breeding. Genetic testing for CEA has recently been developed so that dogs who carry the gene which causes the condition may be prevented from breeding, and thus passing on the defect.

• ENTROPION

Entropion is a condition in which the eyelids fold inward. The eyelid normally protects the eye and ensures that tear fluid is evenly distributed across it. When the eyelid folds inward, this causes the hair to rub on the eye, which affects the tear fluid and results in pain or inflammation that can lead to serious visual impairment. The constant rubbing can cause damage to the cornea which can sometimes even mean loss of the eye. Entropion is more common in certain breeds such as the shar pei, chow-chow, labrador and English bulldog. The condition can be treated with an operation.

• PTOSIS

Ptosis is also a condition affecting the eyelid, which causes the lid to hang over the eye and impair the ability to see. The breeds affected by ptosis include various mastiffs, cocker spaniel and shar pei.

Case history
TROLLI

Trolli has been living with his owner for five years. When his owner got him, he was estimated to be between five and seven years old. He is a Dalmatian, and was re-homed by Dalmatians in Need, Austria, an association which 'liberated' him from the animal refuge in St Margarethen im Burgenland, where, for two-and-a-half years, Trollie had lived in a solitary kennel because he was considered aggressive.

Trolli has a genetic condition and has apparently been completely blind from birth. He has glaucoma and has also developed a cataract in one eye over the past few years. It seems as though the glaucoma causes him pain (increased intra-ocular pressure), and his eyeballs are also slightly enlarged, which is why, for a while, his owner considered having his eyes removed in order to guarantee him freedom from pain. It is very important for Trolli to keep to a strict routine, as he tends to suffer from stress.

Trolli often walks off the lead. In his home territory, he is very self-confident, and even when sometimes there are obstacles in certain places where he would not expect them, he finds his way around. Occasionally he bumps into things, but that only happens when his owner hasn't been attentive enough. He knows the command 'careful!' and slows down and becomes more cautious. He knows his way around the house very well, but when he is excited, such as when a visitor comes, he may bump into something. When he is out on a walk, he always stays near his owner. If he wanders too far away, she calls him. Sometimes she jingles her keys, so that Trolli knows exactly where she is. If it is very windy, he sometimes won't know exactly where she is but misses her by only three or four metres when she calls him.

He is very loving to people; very devoted and in need of lots of cuddles. Strange dogs, however, are unfortunately a big problem. When he and his owner are out for a walk, they take great pains to avoid other dogs, as he gets very agitated when he meets new dogs. He tends to snap wildly in the air, out of stress. If the other dog just sits quietly and lets him sniff it over, there is no problem, though, sadly, other dogs often misunderstand him. Siqua, the second dog in the family, also took a long time to understand Trolli's body language.

He doesn't broadcast very many calming signals. When he doesn't like something, he generally growls immediately, and doesn't often display signals such as yawning or licking his lips (signs of anxiety/nervousness).

When he is excited, for example, when he is starting out on a walk or is going to be fed, Trolli turns round and round and whines.

Passersby either ignore him or ask why he always whines when they set out for a walk. The usual reaction is then pity. To date, only one man has asked why he hasn't been put down. Trolli's favourite game is playing catch with his owner.

Last autumn, Trolli was very ill with acute liver poisoning contracted from a flea collar, and nearly died. His liver values were so bad that the vet at the clinic wanted to put him to sleep immediately.

His owner went with her gut instinct and sought a second opinion and a homeopathic vet was able to save him. This is another example of how important it is to get other opinions. Now, as Trolli is already an elderly gentleman and has also developed a cardiac valvular incompetence, this episode has given him and his owner the gift of a new life together. Trolli probably still has a few enjoyable and exciting years ahead of him and his owner takes care to enjoy their time together, thankful for every moment that she has him.

Chapter 5

Taking a blind dog into your home

Socialisation

When training a dog, it is particularly important to teach him how to deal with normal, everyday events and situations. This means that, whilst still a puppy, your dog should become used to people of both sexes and all ages, and a variety of dogs, both at home and out on walks.

This process is essential for all puppies (once a dog reaches a certain age, socialisation becomes impossible), but even more so for a dog which cannot see. So familiarise your dog at the right time with the largest possible variety of stimuli without overtaxing him. If you take a great deal of time to do this patiently and quietly, you will have a dog who finds it easier to deal with new situations.

Socialisation with people should begin at the age of two weeks, by picking up your dog carefully and handling him gently. A dog that has not been adequately socialised by the age of 12 weeks can develop

problems in this respect that are very hard to correct; the same is true of contact with other dogs.

Spend plenty of time at the right time getting your dog used to other dogs, and show him that his own kind are really fun, so that he doesn't develop a fear of them.

When you take a blind dog or a blind puppy into your home, firstly, get him used to the people that he will be dealing with on a daily basis; ie members of the family. It is important not to overtax him, so don't organise a party to which you have invited all your friends and relatives so that he can get to know them all at once. Your dog would not be able to cope with that and would not have a positive experience from it.

When you have got your dog used to you and your family, invite round your friends and relatives so that your dog can become used to strangers. Make sure that you also invite children and older people, so that your blind dog

experiences every possible type of person. Observe your dog carefully during this process: when does it get too much for him? Perhaps he doesn't want to be stroked? Keep a close eye on him and identify his reactions: when he needs some peace and quiet, leave him alone, but make sure he knows where to find you.

Grooming and handling

Ensure that you also take time at the right point to get your dog used to grooming and being touched and handled. Many dogs dislike being brushed because they are just not used to it, which is why it's important to make this part of your routine right from the start.

Initially, brush your dog gently and affectionately for a couple of seconds, then give him a food reward or play with him – the idea is that he should associate brushing with something pleasant. Make sure that everyone in the family brushes him, too.

Also habituate him to other situations, such as visits to the vet, so that he is used to being held gently and examined. Lift up his flews (the loose flaps of skin on the sides of the upper muzzle that hang to different lengths over the mouth), and gently examine his paw or other part of his body. Always be gentle and careful in your treatment of him so that he never has any reason to mistrust you. Keep these practice sessions short.

Once your dog is happy having you handle him, get your relatives and friends to practice the same thing with him. During these training sessions, don't forget to speak kindly to your dog, to reassure him that you are not a danger. Stop the training session before it gets too much, ie before he begins giving out strong calming signals (yawning, lip-licking), or tries to escape from you. Your dog should always be happy during training sessions and not be made to feel in any way uncomfortable.

At home

Most blind dogs can memorise a complete mental plan of their surroundings in a very short time, but, until your dog has managed this, you can help him, and reduce the risks.

Take a look around your house. Are there any 'traps'? Are there any objects lying around? Try not to leave anything lying on the floor (my blind dog has made me into a very tidy person!). I would also recommend not repositioning anything in your home, as blind dogs feel much happier when everything stays in the same place.

You can help dogs that suffer from night-blindness by using lighting. Energy-saving nightlights are an option; sometimes, a child's nightlight that plugs directly into the socket may be all that is needed. Initially, put these lights in every room in which the dog passes through or spends time. It will not be long before he won't need the lights, but follow your instinct. If I go out for a couple of hours in the evening, I always leave dim lights on for my dogs, who can see enough in terms of contrast for it to be helpful. You can also fix strips of black tape to the corners of walls; if your dog has some residual vision, this will provide a contrast. You can also delineate stairs using this method.

Some owners of blind dogs also use scent marking, but avoid using essential oils as they are very strong and could be unpleasant for your dog.

There are plenty of other simple ways that you can make your dog's everyday life easier. If you travel with

Make a place in your home where your blind dog can relax and feel secure.

your dog and have to stay in an unfamiliar hotel room, simply cut a lemon in half and wipe it once over the door frame. This will help your dog get his bearings. Of course, you do have to train him to understand this means of orientation, so practice at home: wipe the lemon over the door frame and tap on it with your fingers. Your dog will quickly learn to associate the odour with a door.

There are also methods for floor and sound marking. For example, you could place rugs at the bottom and top of the stairs and create a path of rugs leading to food and water bowls.

Avoid moving your furniture at all costs as this confuses a blind dog. If you do have to do this,

lead your dog slowly up to and around the repositioned object; it would be unkind to simply let him crash into it. In any given situation, he needs you more than he needs anything else, so ensure that you are there for him, and provide as much support as possible. Don't forget that your dog has to create a three-dimensional plan in his head, which takes some time. Furthermore, his bed and feeding/watering area should never be moved under any circumstances.

When you take a blind dog into your home, it is advisable initially to pad any sharp corners and edges. Put protective foam coverings or similar on the corners and edges of tables – particularly when they are at the dog's eye level. Sharp corners and edges are dangerous, and your dog could injure himself whilst still unfamiliar with his surroundings.

Take care to ensure that your dog doesn't suffer any bad experiences right from the start, such as being startled by something unexpected. There's one opportunity only to acquire a good first impression, and your dog's needs to be positive! Many blind dogs are confused and nervous in strange surroundings, so it is imperative you provide a peaceful, stress-free atmosphere. Keep the dog on a loose lead and talk kindly to him – a lead will often give a feeling of security. Walk your dog slowly around each room and carefully introduce him to and around all the items of furniture.

In the garden

The same basic principles apply in the garden, although there are, of course, more dangers outside, in particular when it is windy and the weather is bad, as this will mean that conditions underfoot are poor.

Ensure that your garden is properly fenced. If your dog gets out and is wandering around with no idea of where he is, the consequences can be very dire. Of course, this is not a good scenario even for a sighted dog, but significantly more dangerous for a blind dog.

Fence off hazardous parts of your garden. To do this, you need to view the garden from your companion's perspective. Are there shrubs with sharp thorns or branches at the height of your dog's eyes? If so,

fence them off, as they represent a serious injury risk. When it is windy, your dog may, perhaps, be more likely to bump into things than when conditions are still. This is normal, as all his other senses will be compromised.

You can also install a dog flap. This is particularly advisable for older dogs, as they can then decide for themselves if they want to go out. Don't forget to teach your blind dog how to use it, though!

Walks

Sometimes it can be helpful if you wear a bell when you go out for a walk. Just *how* useful this is, depends on the individual dog, as it can make some anxious. Find out what *your* dog prefers. The most important aid to his orientation is still your voice.

If you have another dog which the blind dog uses as a guide, you could consider attaching a small bell to the sighted dog as long as this does not cause stress.

Trolli, the blind Dalmatian, lives with the pointer cross Siqua. When Trolli is off the lead, he relies heavily on Siqua as a guide, so their owner attached a small bell to Siqua's harness. When they are out, they run so closely together that you would scarcely notice that one of them can't see.

Which takes us back to another important point: blind dogs depend a great deal on other dogs in the group. If you keep a blind dog, consider getting a self-assured second dog. Of course, you shouldn't get a second dog for this reason alone, but because you want one! Your second dog will also be an individual and perhaps have totally different needs to your first dog. (Apart from the basic ones such as food, water and exercise, of course.)

Whatever the case, organise your walks so that they are stress-free, relaxed and restful, and 'show' your blind dog things during the walk, so that he knows you are looking after him. For example, you can place a tasty treat on a park bench and

dog off the lead depends on how well he follows you and how good he is at getting his bearings. Don't keep changing the routes of your walks, but instead have two or three different walks that you can stick to if your dog becomes stressed or anxious when on unfamiliar territory. Placing your dog under stress is, after all, not the objective of a walk. However, keep your walks full of variety as there is nothing more boring than a monotonous walk. My

Hattie on holiday in France.

'show' it to your dog with the words "Look at what I've found!" Your dog will definitely enjoy this, and doing exciting and fun activities with you will increase his self-confidence.

Whether you can let your blind

blind Elliott has four routes; they are all very different and the one we choose depends on the weather and the time of day. (And also on my mood to some extent!) You certainly shouldn't confine your dog to the house and garden because he is blind and never take him for a walk. Always take him out and focus on him. You will notice for yourself how well the dog copes with his environment, and can decide on the basis of this how to arrange his everyday life.

In principle, Elliott would get on with virtually all dogs if they could

Only you can decide if it is advisable to label your dog in this way, but, whatever else you do, you should attach a small bag or container to his harness containing important information such as the fact that he is blind and, of course, your name and telephone number and any other necessary details. If you do decide on a bib

Elliott wearing his 'bib.'

approach each other slowly. But because some dog owners don't have their dogs on leads and they are allowed to rush up to us, Elliott sometimes wears a bib indicating that he is blind. This protects him from people who want to touch him and also (but not always) from free-ranging dogs.

for your dog, don't forget that this will attract attention and you find yourself having to answer questions, as people will often talk to you about this when you are on a walk. Consider whether you want to deal with this. I feel it is a good thing as it will inform others about blind dogs and also demonstrate that they can be easily integrated into home life. I made Elliott's bib myself out of a mountain rescue harness, which was given to him by a very kind neighbour.

Meeting other dogs and people on walks

When you go out for a walk with your dog, use signal words to let him know that dogs or people are approaching. Inform your dog so that he is prepared. Of course, your dog will probably know before you do that a dog is approaching, but he will certainly be reassured that you are communicating this to him, because you are out and about together as a team. It's always possible that he might be busy and not have noticed that a dog is approaching. If this is the case, your warning means that he can prepare himself and will not be surprised.

If a dog comes bounding up and makes no effort to run around you or to slow down, you can make it do so by placing yourself about a metre in front of your dog, in-between him and the strange dog. Ensure that you stay calm and in control and don't forget that you are responsible for your dog.

Basic compliance

Elliott was trained using audio and visual signs. I know my dog very well, but the crucial issue is that he knows me even better. He always knows what I expect of him in certain situations, and that makes our life together very simple and predictable. Most importantly, because he is a very insecure dog,

this predictability gives him security. Of course, even the most patient dog goes 'deaf' when his humans constantly want something from him, so try not to do this.

The reason I use visual signals with him is for my benefit; I want to broadcast what I want from him with absolute clarity, to make it easier for him. My dog can sense when I am confident about what I want. Visual signals give me more of an air of certainty in terms of body language and a means of expression.

All owners of blind dogs that I have met use both audio and visual signals, and this may be because we humans are very much primarily reliant on our sense of sight, and in today's society so much is designed to appeal to this particular sense that visual signals are an automatic response for us.

The most crucial factor in training a blind dog is, of course, speech. It is the key aid to the dog finding his way. So you need to learn to use speech correctly; ie so that your dog understands what you want him to do. In general, higher sounds will generate positive attention from a dog. In addition, a dog hears between 4 and 20 times better than a human, so it is really not necessary to speak especially loudly to him; in the wild, animals communicate with each other very quietly when the topic is something important, such as enemies or food, which is the reason why we are more likely to get our dog's attention using a quiet rather than a loud voice.

It is certainly the right approach to talk more to your blind dog, but

Case history
EMI

Emi and Katrin met in an animal refuge in France. Emi was found on the street in a very poor condition with an ingrown collar. The assumption was that she was a watchdog, disposed of as she couldn't effectively guard any more because of her age.

Katrin went into the kennel and tried to make contact, but Emi was completely apathetic and didn't react to anything. She could hardly walk and her eyes were crusted and inflamed.

Katrin took her to a vet, who diagnosed several tumours, drastic undernourishment, fleas, a fungal infection and blindness. Under the circumstances, it is not possible to determine Emi's exact age, but she is thought to be between twelve and fifteen years old.

Katrin housed Emi in her conservatory, where she had direct access to the garden and was kept apart from her other two dogs, Janosch and Lila, for the time being. The dogs could sniff and get to know each other through the dog guard, without any of them feeling harassed. At this point, Emi still wasn't reacting to anything at all, so the suspicion arose that she might also be deaf.

Emi was frightened whenever she was touched, although, as she could scarcely walk, Katrin had to help her when she got herself stuck in a dead-end. Katrin put a soft, anti-slip floor covering down in the conservatory so that Emi could move around. All the danger zones in the garden, such as the pond, were fenced off.

After a while, Emi was able to get her bearings to some extent, and began to roam endlessly and pointlessly round the garden. Katrin tried to gradually get Emi used to her other dogs, and, whilst there were no problems with Janosch, Lila tended to feel threatened more quickly, as Emi registered her presence either too late or not at all, and this irritated Lila. Thankfully, after a while, Lila also accepted Emi's erratic approaches. Emi does not climb steps, so the other dogs can retreat to the upper floor when they need some peace. None of the dogs was ever shut out, although Katrin often asked the dogs to wait for her at the door, which all of them accepted.

Over time, Emi began to show a greater range of reactions to stimuli, and even regained some of her vision; her ophthalmitis (inflammation of the eye) cleared up completely. She perceives movement, walks around the garden, sniffs, digs, and holds her face up to the wind.

She is less frightened when she is touched and can also enjoy the odd stroke. Katrin and her

husband continue to approach Emi from the right as she apparently sees better on this side, and they don't touch her until she has recognised them.

When Emi began to leave the conservatory and venture into the house, Katrin and her husband laid out carpet runners for her to follow so that she can go into every room, which she likes doing.

Seven months ago, the vet gave Emi only days to live, but she is still going strong today. She leads an active life, is curious, and looks forward to every new day.

this does not mean that you should chatter to him endlessly.

Equipment

This subject is very close to my heart as I have come across some almost unbelievable equipment in the books written by so-called 'experts.' All sorts of things ranging from spiked collars and choke chains, to poles with which blind dogs are led to enable them to be guided 'better' and 'more safely.' In fact, you really don't need anything more than a properly-fitting chest harness, a three metre lead, and tasty treats that your dog enjoys.

The chest harness has significant health and psychological advantages over a collar: it is preferable in health terms because accidental jerks on the lead – for instance if the blind or sight-impaired dog is frightened and jumps to one side – will not result in damage to the spine, larynx or trachea. The pressure exerted by pulling on the collar is also known to contribute to an increase in intra-ocular pressure, which can be counterproductive in the case of some eye conditions (see page 21).

A harness is preferable in psychological terms also because negative associations can be made more quickly with a collar than with a chest harness. For example, your dog can be much more relaxed about making contact with other dogs whilst wearing a chest harness, as pressure from the collar is unpleasant and can increase negative feelings (aggression), or even initiate them, which will then be associated with the 'meeting a strange dog' scenario. This is particularly important when your dog is insecure and pulls towards or away from another dog, as the human at the other end of the lead is then involuntarily giving out incorrect information via the pressure on his neck, which could put a blind or visually-impaired dog in an unpleasant and perhaps even dangerous situation. The dog must really be able to rely on the information received from his human.

In urban areas, it is perhaps advisable to use a shorter lead (two metres), or shorten your three metre lead. It may also be worth getting five and ten metre leads to use depending on the terrain covered.

Once again, I can only advise you to observe your dog and see which lead length suits him best.

Steer clear of any training aids which harm the dog or cause him any shock, pain or discomfort; not only are these unnecessary and cruel, they are also counter-productive in any situation, as your dog will quickly come to fear your training sessions. Whatever it is that you want him to learn, teach him kindly without using force or pressure. When you have built a relationship of mutual trust, love and respect, your dog will be an obedient animal that you can let off the lead in spite of his disability. All you need is plenty of patience and love, and possibly a good dog trainer to provide some help.

Don't forget that the key element is your relationship with one another. Your dog is a reflection of you and how you are. If you are nervous, unsure and anxious, your dog will probably be the same …

Chapter 6

Calming signals and stress

Blind dogs will also display calming signals when they feel uncomfortable and are finding a situation unpleasant. For example, observe a dog that is called by her owner in a stern voice and you will probably see the dog display a range of calming signals to pacify the owner. Most dogs will look away and their pace will become slower and slower; they are not doing this to provoke their owner, but to appease him or her. Most frequently seen calming signals are, for instance, yawning or licking the lips, pawing or blinking. Watch your dog to check if she is sending any signals that could indicate to you she is uneasy, indicating that, perhaps, you should remove her from this situation. On no account should you ignore calming signals.

Some blind dogs – for example, Trolli, who is mentioned earlier – skip this stage of communication and growl immediately they feel uncomfortable. This is not serious, and the reason for it is probably

that when they were a puppy they were not able to watch other dogs and learn how they communicate. Dogs that were not born blind generally exhibit the full repertoire of calming signals. Blind dogs often become stressed more quickly than sighted dogs, which is also entirely normal as they are missing one of their senses and can't observe their environment in the same way as sighted dogs. Stress can also arise for a variety of different reasons: fear, over-excited play, unrest in the family or generally in the household; as the result of an excess of exercise or training, pain or illness.

It is, of course, fine for a dog to experience stress from time to time – some stress is necessary to survive – but continuously high levels of stress are not good for any creature. Indeed, the opposite is true, as chronic stress causes physical and mental problems such as high blood pressure and gastric ulcers. A dog suffering from chronic stress can also suffer from migraines, digestive

Shila is panting, which could be stress-induced.

problems, poor quality sleep, and other debilitating ailments.

Don't forget that many things will cause a blind dog much more stress than they would a sighted dog, and that she may also have a lower stress tolerance level. When a dog is really stressed, she cannot even send any appeasement signals and just reacts by displaying associated symptoms. Watch out for stereotypical behaviour, such as turning in circles, which I have observed in several blind dogs. Other symptoms are barking, whining, trembling, snapping in the air, expanded pupils, paw-biting, teeth-chattering, sweating paws and excessive digging or scratching at the ground. (This list is not exhaustive.)

If your dog is panting a great deal it could definitely be the case that she is extremely stressed and finding her current situation – unfamiliar surroundings, for example – overwhelming. It is important to always look at the bigger picture, though, because, of course, this could just be a sign that she is hot! There can be many reasons why a dog might bark a lot; it may be because of a stress-related problem, or simply because she belongs to a breed that is more inclined to bark.

Always adapt your behaviour to

suit your dog's learning speed and stage of life. If your dog doesn't cope well with large crowds of people, avoid taking her to crowded places. You can slowly acclimatise her to new places, but always go at a pace that she finds comfortable.

Remember that when your dog is stressed, she cannot obey your commands any more because she loses the ability to concentrate. It may also be the case that she won't accept any treats as she is too anxious to eat. Take note of this and respect her feelings; on no account should you tell her off, just simply remove her from the stressful situation.

Chapter 7

Basic commands

The extent to which a blind dog does as you ask depends, of course, on how well he did this before he went blind. If he wasn't compliant and was unsure about following basic commands when he could see, he's not going to be any better now that he's blind. In this regard it may be helpful to find a good dog trainer, but if you do, just concentrate on the essentials and take note of your gut feelings. Don't allow anything that makes you feel uncomfortable or that you can't justify.

It's true to say that trust is a prerequisite for basic obedience; your dog will not follow your commands reliably if he doesn't trust you. This means that commands must always be issued kindly, otherwise your dog will learn that commands are sometimes something good and sometimes something bad. Your dog should be obedient to you because he finds it fun and because he wants to please you by obeying, not because he is afraid of you

There are a few things that you can teach your dog to make his everyday life easier. When you bring a blind dog home for the first time, leave him to settle in for the first few weeks – your new friend will probably have enough on his plate familiarising himself with his new environment and new family. It generally takes a couple of weeks for a dog's stress levels to reduce and for him to settle. Don't begin training until your dog knows that you are his 'pack.' Always teach your dog commands in series, ie make sure that he has completely understood one command before moving on to the next. This will prevent him from becoming confused.

It is better for your dog to know a few commands and to obey these reliably than to know numerous commands which he confuses, or in which he is unreliable in terms of obeying. Always remember that dogs are living creatures and not machines. There is never a cast-iron guarantee for anything and, for this reason, your dog – even if he is very obedient – should always be on a lead when close to a busy road or some other danger. This will provide peace of mind for you and your dog: I'm always seeing dogs being walked off-lead near roads, and it is obvious that both dog and owner are tense, the owner constantly hissing "heel" and intimidating the animal, who is concentrating all his efforts on not straying one pace from his owner's side. That's not a recipe for a pleasant and relaxed life together! Forget the old clichés about how a dog can only be happy if he's always off the lead. It is certainly true that a dog needs exercise, but what matters to your dog is your attitude and what that tells him; if you're always thinking "poor dog" when he is on a lead, this will be communicated to him and he will feel disadvantaged. If you radiate confidence and an aura of well-being, on the other hand, your dog won't have a problem either.

If training is not going well on any particular day, defer it to the next, as your dog may well be having a bad day or simply not feel like it. Only ever practice when your dog wants to participate and not because you feel that you have to. Instead, you can play or simply sit together in a field with the sun on your faces. Don't forget to praise him each time he achieves or attempts the commands.

"Look" with audible signal

"Look" is the command for recalling your dog to you. Why am I calling a blind dog with "Look" when he can't see anything? It's important when choosing a word to use for the recall command that you avoid one which is commonly used in everyday conversation. "Here" or "Come" are therefore not recommended as commands as they are used much too frequently in general everyday interchanges.

Always use the same command, because your dog needs to link a specific word with a specific action. It is important that blind dogs always know what is expected of them so have only one command for a particular action.

Practice the command initially in an environment with very few distractions, perhaps at home, with a treat in your hand and calling your dog by his name. When you have his attention and he is looking in your direction, say "Look" in an encouraging voice and praise him as soon as he moves in your direction.

When he gets close to you, help him to locate you, for example, by clapping your hands quietly. Another option is to click your tongue. Give your dog his treat. It will only take him a little time to understand that "Look" followed by an audible guide signal means that he should come to you and he will receive a nice reward.

POTENTIAL PROBLEMS

It could be that your dog is not coming when you call because he can't locate you. Try and view it from his point of view and pay attention to how you are communicating – take particular care with your audible signal so that your dog can precisely pinpoint where you are.

Be confident that your dog will follow your command to come to you – wherever he may be.

It could also be the case that you are calling your dog too much and that he simply doesn't want to cooperate any more. Consider how often you call your dog when you are out for a walk with him and how often he doesn't come to you.

Owners often make the mistake of calling unnecessarily and far too often, so that the command loses meaning. Also ensure that you don't use the command without due consideration for the situation and environment/obstacles, etc. Take care not to over-practice and quit whilst you're ahead!

"Careful"

"Careful" lets your dog know there are obstacles that he needs to avoid. Teach him to walk around either to the left or the right, because trying to teach both will confuse him. You could, of course, teach two commands: one for turning right to avoid an obstacle and one for turning left, in which case take care to teach your dog one command first, ensuring that he can reliably obey that one before teaching the second.

Put your dog on a loose lead and walk around for a little while. Before you get to an obstacle (a bag, for example), which you have previously placed, decrease your pace, say "Careful," and walk an obvious arc around the obstacle. You can also let your dog touch the obstacle first. Repeat this several times and gradually increase the degree of difficulty.

POTENTIAL PROBLEMS

It may be that you are going too fast in both walking speed and degree of difficulty. It is important that you do not allow your dog to hurt himself when doing this, or he will come to associate the command with an unpleasant experience and become afraid and fearful of what lies in his way. With this command, progress slowly and at a pace your dog is comfortable with; if he shows signs of becoming tired, or anxious about the unseen obstacles he is being asked to negotiate, stop immediately, reassure him and then do something nice, like play or massage/stroke him.

"Stop"

Stop means coming to an immediate and complete standstill, though in what position is not important. Your dog should remain in that spot until released by your next command. This can save a blind dog's life, and his grasp and obedience of this command should be 100 per cent. A certain amount of thought must go into deciding at which point to use a particular command, especially when you are out walking and scanning the terrain ahead for possible problems. In many situations, you may not have much

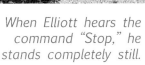

When Elliott hears the command "Stop," he stands completely still.

time in which to consider whether it is better to use "Careful" or "Stop" In addition, your dog must have mastered the commands sufficiently in order to carry them out correctly. What is paramount is that you don't forget that you are your dog's eyes; you must be able to communicate to him that he could be about to get into a dangerous situation and he must believe you.

Put your dog on a loose lead and walk around for a little while, then halt and say "Stop." As soon as he does, reward him with a treat and praise him in a warm voice. Before you continue, give him a second command which tells him that he can now continue: your dog cannot know how long he should spend in this position. "And go" makes a good release command.

Gradually increase the degree of difficulty. When your dog has understood the basic principle, try it without a lead somewhere where he cannot come to harm.

Potential problems

Be consistent when teaching the stop command, as this is the only way to guarantee your blind dog's safety. If he always gets up and begins to move before you give him the release command, you may be asking him to retain that position longer than he can tolerate. Go back a couple of steps in your training and only increase very gradually the time that your dog spends motionless.

"Slowly"
"Slowly" is a very important command, particularly for those dogs with some residual vision. Once again, practice with your dog on a loose lead. Walk around for a while and gradually reduce speed whilst saying "Slooooowly." If you draw the word out, the majority of dogs will react by slowing down simply to the sound of the word. Again, don't forget to praise your dog so that he knows he is doing the right thing.

POTENTIAL PROBLEMS
If your dog doesn't understand straight away what is required, try making the difference more noticeable between your initial speed and when you begin slowing so that he can differentiate between the two more readily. Practice in a quiet location with no distractions and with your dog on a loose lead.

"Steps"
"Steps" is probably one of the most important commands for a blind dog. You should introduce one command for going up steps and one for going down.

Practice the command by saying the signal word and carefully negotiating a step with your dog; ie take the dog to the step and let him check it out. You can also knock on the step to tell him there is a flight of stairs. As soon as you have reached the top of the stairs, say something like "Finished" so that he knows there are no more steps.

If you have steps at home, your dog will learn very quickly how many there are and where they are, and memorise a plan of his surroundings. In this case, you will no longer need to give the commands as he will know where the steps/stairs are.

Getting into the car
It is important for everyday life to teach your blind dog a command to prepare him for getting into the car; make sure you also teach him a command for getting out! Even when a dog can see, it is very dangerous to let him jump out of the car unchecked.

My dog, Elliott, is conditioned to the sound of the remote locking and unlocking of the car, which is something he has taught himself. He has learnt that the noise means he will immediately hear the command "Jump." At the same time I pat the car seat with the flat of my hand.

Initially, it is sufficient if you physically help your dog in and out of the car. Hold his chest harness lightly and help him in. Give him a treat for getting in and do the same when he gets out. Don't forget to speak to your dog kindly whilst doing these manoeuvres.

"Go right/Go left"
Few blind dogs like being touched by strangers, so you need to protect your dog from the well-meaning and loving actions of strangers if he is likely to object to them. It has happened more than once that, whilst out and about in town with Elliott, a stranger has reached down

Elliott has no problem negotiating the spiral staircase.

whilst going past to give my dog a pat on the head. Just put yourself in the blind animal's position to understand how this might seem to him.

This is why I have introduced the commands "Go right" and "Go left," to be used when we don't have the option of avoiding strangers. If someone is coming towards us, I use myself as a buffer: I know my dog, but I don't know the person who is approaching us. I say "Elliott, go left!" and snap the fingers of my left hand at the height of my upper thigh; Elliott then changes position to my left side. The same applies for "Go right!", as he then knows that he must change position to be on my right side. It is important that you use a release command ("And go") to resolve the position commands, as the dog doesn't know when the manoeuvre is finished. If you don't use a release command, he will make his own decision and, perfectly understandably, end the manoeuvre when he sees fit.

In order to teach the command "Go left," call your dog to you and have a treat in your left hand. Walk for a while with him and the treat on your left side. He will detect the treat in your left hand and will be walking close by your left side. Repeat the command several times, then stand still, give him the treat and use the release command "And go." Repeat this exercise several times and when the dog has understood and produces a reliable response to the command, do the same with "Go right."

POTENTIAL PROBLEMS

Don't give the treat until he is standing still, otherwise you are rewarding him for walking slowly. However, he should make the connection between his position (on either your right or left side) with the command.

"Sit"

Sit is a command that you can perhaps use for your blind dog. Many dogs find it easier to stay in one place for a short time when first they have been told to "Sit," although you should never leave him to sit for longer than he can cope with. You should never give the "Sit" command and then leave him alone somewhere (eg outside a supermarket). I really only use "Sit" when I'm hiding a toy which Elliott then has to look for. If I leave him to stand, he always walks a few steps as soon as he doesn't have my attention any more.

To teach your dog the "Sit"

command, with him standing in front of you, take a treat in your hand and hold it over the back of his head. Catching the scent from this direction, he will sit in order to get closer to the treat; at the moment his bottom touches the ground, say "Sit" and give him the treat, praising him as you do. Repeat this exercise three times and then stop; never practice more than three times in a row. When you are sure your dog has understood what you want from him, try using just the signal word. Don't forget to use the release command "And go" when you have finished the exercise and your dog can stand up again.

POTENTIAL PROBLEMS

If you hold the treat too high, the dog may attempt to jump to get it. If this happens, don't scold him because it is your mistake; hold the treat lower over his head.

If your dog constantly stands up before the exercise is finished, it may be that you are making it too difficult or uncomfortable for him. Try making the exercises shorter.

Everyday conversations

As already mentioned, you should spend more time speaking to your blind dog than would be usual if he was sighted, although don't chatter at him incessantly. Tell him what you are doing, when you are, for example, preparing his food, or when you are getting ready to go for a walk, so that he knows what is coming next. This will be a great help to him in dealing with everyday life.

Sari is deaf and Elliottt is blind, but both dogs have learned the "Sit" command.

Free

Some owners have a command for 'running free,' to let their dog know that there are no obstacles and he can run around as much as he likes without fear. I think this is a bit problematic, because it means that whenever there is no obstacle I should give this command. I would have to give this command constantly, because I am always looking ahead to ensure that there is nothing in Elliott's way.

I can imagine introducing something of this sort if a dog is unsure and not confident about walking, although I think that a few cheering, encouraging and kindly words should be enough to reassure your dog that he has nothing to worry about because you are looking after him.

Case history
Dodger

Dodger is a fourteen-year-old German shepherd cross who lives with his family in Germany. He came from an animal refuge, to which he was taken when he was two years old. One year later, his current owner took him into her home.

Dodger is now nearly deaf and has lost almost 90 per cent of his sight. His owner noticed the first signs of cloudiness in his right eye three or four years ago, but there were no discernible problems with this. However, he then began to follow his owner very closely wherever she went, and showed increasing signs of anxiety when she left the room and he didn't know where she was. He would then scent-search every room - and still does this today.

These days, both of Dodger's eyes are cloudy. He recognises body movement from a distance, but if a hand is held up close to his right eye, there is no reaction at all. When he is in his usual environment, he has no trouble finding his way around, and does not bump into the furniture. If there are objects on the floor, however, he will sometimes knock them over or tread on them.

When out on a walk, Dodger always stays behind his owner. He now only reacts to very loud noises, although, even then, he often looks in the wrong direction, because he can't tell where the sound is coming from.

Dodger lives with the mastiffs Camelot and Rusty and the Belgian Malinois bitch, Marlie, although doesn't use any of the other dogs as a guide. Dodger doesn't have any problems with Rusty and Marlie, but has a more complicated relationship with Camelot because they are afraid of each other. Dodger can't hear any more when a dog is approaching him from behind or from the side, and, because one day he didn't hear Camelot's approach, he was surprised when he suddenly appeared behind him, and snapped at him. Since then, the dogs have kept their distance and try to avoid each other. If they do happen to meet, they stare straight ahead and turn their heads away very sharply. Their owner helps them out of this situation by standing between them. Luckily, the dogs have a great deal of space at home, which enables them to avoid each other, and have people around who deal with them in a manner that is both prudent and farsighted.

Dodger has never been particularly interested in strange dogs. However, it is now very important because of his visual impairment that his owner warns him about the approach of strange dogs. If he has enough time and distance, meetings with other dogs pass off peacefully, but if he is surprised, he can react by snapping.

Dodger uses all types of calming signals and has not forgotten anything in this respect. He licks his lips, yawns, turns his head away and just makes brief contact. He keeps his distance, sniffs about and busies himself with territorial marking in order to demonstrate that he does not represent any danger.

Dodger's owner gives him a great deal of support in everyday life. He has an entry assistance device with side barriers for the car, and also receives plenty of physical support from his humans. In an unfamiliar environment, they make an effort to stay close by his side, if that is what he wants. Otherwise, he is often on the lead, as this is a connection with his owner which provides him with security. Unfortunately, Dodger has advanced hip dysplasia and limited mobility, which means that the lead limits his freedom of movement. When he is off the lead, he can choose whether to walk slowly or quickly, whereas when on the lead he feels he has to hurry to keep up.

His human carers ensure that no one approaches him from behind or from the right-hand side, as this terrifies him. He has a lot of physical contact with his humans, who also manage to secure him enough space in any possible conflict situation which his impaired vision has prevented him from assessing in time.

Dodger is supported by great people, whom he can trust, and who help him to manage and feel comfortable with life, despite his visual disability.

Chapter 8

Introducing your blind dog to the rest of the group

If you have several dogs at home, ideally these dogs will form a stable 'group' (sometimes wrongly referred to as a 'pack,' which is a family group; ie parent animals with their offspring). Only a few people actually keep a pack; most have a group of unrelated dogs. If you want to integrate a blind dog with your existing group, there are a number of issues to consider.

The most important thing is to ensure that your blind dog gets to know your other dogs in a quiet place, preferably before you actually take her home. If you have several dogs, it is better to let the blind dog get to know them one at a time, so that the process doesn't tax her.

One way of doing this might be to take them on a quiet walk with which the blind dog is already familiar. It is important that you don't let the dogs rush at each other, so keep both/all on a loose lead initially.

Ask someone to assist you with the introduction, because this will help to create a calm and peaceful atmosphere. Give your helper instructions in advance about what they need to do; there's nothing worse than having to call out or shout instructions during such an important meeting, as this will disrupt the atmosphere. If there's no other way of doing it, consider communicating via mobile/cell phone.

The first meeting is very important as this is the only chance to create a good, positive first impression.

I recommend having your helper go ahead; this should be someone that your first dog knows and likes, and is happy to go with without fuss – she needs to feel comfortable, too. Then walk with your blind dog some way behind them. Make the distance between you generous and reduce it gradually as the dogs become more comfortable. The aim is for them to eventually walk next to each other in a relaxed manner so that they can get to know each other. Always keep the leads loose so that you do not create any tension.

Repeat these walks on neutral ground several times. You will soon see whether your dogs can identify each other by smell!

When your blind dog has got to know your other dogs during these relaxed communal walks, you can begin to take her home with you. It is not a bad idea to let the blind dog get to know her new home without the other dogs being present, so that she can sniff around in peace and concentrate on her surroundings, but avoid presenting her with too many stimuli at once. When she has familiarised himself with her new home, take all of your dogs for a walk (after all, she knows them all now) and afterwards all go home together.

Ensure that your blind dog has some quiet places where she can be by herself, and take special care to avoid any potential conflict situations. If one of your dogs defends resources, such as her toys, remove the toys so that friction does not develop between the animals. If you are not sure that all the animals will eat peacefully together, keep them separate when feeding them.

It is also important that the dogs have sufficient opportunity to give each

other a wide berth, so avoid any bottleneck situations and enable them all to have enough space to feel comfortable.

If you have a dog who is very 'busy' and you have the feeling that your blind dog needs some peace and quiet (or the other way around), don't ask the dogs to go to their beds as this will only cause stress and upset. When nervous or agitated, if it helps them to move about, sitting or remaining still will only exacerbate the situation. As a general rule, movement helps relieve stress. A child's safety gate can be useful here because it allows all of the dogs to see/smell and be near each other, but also have their own

A child's safety gate can be used to physically separate the group, but still allow them to see and smell each other.

space. Pay close attention to calming signals and symptoms of stress in all the dogs and take action as appropriate.

It is normal for dogs to take some time to adjust to each other, as misunderstandings between the animals can frequently arise at the beginning, and the sighted dogs have to learn to communicate with the blind dog. For instance, the blind dog may 'stare' at the sighted dogs, who can interpret this as a threat. If this happens, standing between the dogs will defuse the tension in the situation and your dogs will also learn that you are assuming responsibility – which is very important.

It may also happen that, at first, your blind dog will walk into the sighted dogs or stumble over them, which the sighted dogs will perceive as very impolite. Monitor how the animals deal with it. If they shake themselves and carry on, perhaps they are shrugging off their irritation and there won't be a problem, but ensure that these situations do not generate and build tension. If you feel that all of the dogs have had enough for the moment, make time and space for them to enjoy some peace and quiet. Never send your dogs to bed as a punishment; their bed should be somewhere where they feel at ease and not a place with negative associations.

Eventually, your group should learn to relax together, just as Hubble and Immie did ...

Always remember that stress can be detrimental to the vision of a visually-impaired dog, so, it is particularly important to ensure her well-being. Also be aware that feeding can play an important role in this.

All differences were forgotten at bathtime, as the three members of this group – Hattie, Hubble and Immie – were united in their dislike of it!

Case history
SHILA

Shila was already eleven years old when Anne and Dietmar adopted her from the animal refuge. She is probably a mix of hovawart, border collie and cocker spaniel. Her previous owners obviously weren't that concerned about her health and wellbeing, as at that point Shila was an extremely overweight dog who spent her time standing at the fence barking hysterically at passers-by. In the animal refuge, efforts had been made to get her weight under control with half-size portions of special diet food for older dogs. The first time she came to her new owners' house, she looked all around it and then lay down very deliberately in front of the bed. She obviously wanted to stay!

Shila's eyesight had deteriorated due to her age and she had heart and joint problems.

Her calming signals generally consist of licking her flews and yawning. In comparison to most dogs, she holds eye contact for a considerable length of time, which may be because of her collie heritage, but could also be learned behaviour from the time when she was suffering her temporary bout of bad eyesight. Because Shila's eyesight quickly improved, as soon as she moved into her new home, she was put on a raw food diet which resulted in progressive improvement in her overall health and wellbeing. Her health problems and her visual impairment became less and less significant and Shila became ever fitter. After Shila had spent a year eating raw food and enjoying a wide variety of exercise, the vet to whom Anne and Dietmar had been taking her declared the dog's heart to be completely healthy, and her eyesight has improved so that she now sees reasonably well. Shila is now fifteen years and four months old but doesn't behave like an old dog at all. In spite of her age and associated aches and pains, she is always cheerful and up to all sorts of mischief.

Shila languished for a whole year in the animal refuge before she was able to find a home, because people were put off by her age. But she is a great dog: incredibly clever and very handsome, who learns many new things every day. Anne and Dietmar benefit from her wisdom and experience, as well as the joy she brings them.

Don't overlook older dogs, because they, too, deserve a home with people who love them. And in return you will have their undying gratitude.

Chapter 9

Games to play at home

In principle, you can play the same games with blind dogs that you can with sighted dogs. They can even chase balls, which many people think is impossible. There are many ways of occupying a blind dog appropriately and having a lot of fun together!

Hunting for a toy

Elliott has developed the skill of hunting for toys to an advanced level. He waits in a room and I hide a toy – usually his Kong™ or his dinosaur toy. Your dog must not, of course, hear where you go. Over time, Elliott has got so good at this that I now have to think up really difficult hiding places: in the oven, in the washing machine, or outside the front door. We vary things so that the game doesn't get boring. For instance, he had to learn to open kitchen cupboards and now I can also hide the toys in there. He sits down in front of the cupboard, I say "Open it!" and he pulls on a cord to open the door. Use of the "Open it!" command is important, as he shouldn't get the idea

Elliott and his duck.

to open cupboards when I'm not around. If you do have a dog that takes advantage of your absence by emptying your cupboards, it's advisable to remove the cord when you have finished playing the game.

In order to teach your dog to hunt for a toy, he first of all has to learn what his toy is called. So, if he has to look for a duck, start like this: take the duck and give the dog a playful nudge with it. When he begins to take an interest, ie pick up the duck in his mouth, say "duck" and give him plenty of praise. Repeat this a few times. When you think your dog has understood what this is all about, progress to the next step and place the duck in front of him. Say "duck." He will search the floor for the duck and will find it immediately, and it's important that

he does because he really needs to experience plenty of success at the beginning. Later, you can go a step further and place the duck further away, until you finally get to the point of really hiding it and then introduce the "Find the duck" command.

Distinguishing toys

Another game is distinguishing between toys. You can teach your dog to do this by following the initial few steps detailed above. It is important to ensure that you don't teach your dog the name of a new toy until he is 100 per cent certain about the previous one, so that he doesn't become confused; he needs to have made the link between the toy's name and the toy itself before you move on to the next one.

Kong™ provides entertainment and stimulation.

At Christmas Hattie made short work of opening her presents!

Cartons and packages

The carton is another nice game idea. Stuff a small carton with scrunched-up newspaper with treats mixed in it (there should also be some 'blanks' amongst it, ie wrappers without treats). Your dog will have great fun busily fishing around in the carton to retrieve the treats. You can also create packages made out of folded newspapers held together with string which contain a surprise, such as a chewy toy, a biscuit, or something similar. Start off with very simple packages so that he doesn't get frustrated. At the beginning, just wrap the newspapers together very loosely, until he has understood the principle of the game.

Treat trail and treat hunt

Lay a trail of treats for your dog which leads to something really special. Place the treats some distance apart and lead your dog to the first one, then knock on the ground and say "Find treats!"

You can also play this inside by hiding treats all round your house or flat, so that he has to hunt for them.

If you have more than one dog they can play this game together (assuming they have no problems with sharing food). Turn out the lights so that your sighted dogs don't have an unfair advantage.

Treat hunting!

Learning a trick

It's perfectly okay to teach your blind dog tricks as long as he enjoys it. Most dogs like learning new tricks and are very proud to show them to their two-legged friends. Learning a trick is fun and gives the dog a bit of a challenge. He has to think about what you want from him and work together with you, which is important for his self-confidence, particularly in the case of an insecure canine.

The abilities of blind dogs are on a par with sighted dogs in most ways, and they can learn an unlimited number of tricks.

For example, you can teach your blind dog to shake hands ...

SHAKING HANDS

Hold a treat in your hand, make a fist and hold it out in front of your dog. He will probably try to get to it with his muzzle first. Ignore this attempt and keep your hand closed until he lifts his paw and touches your fist. Say the word "shake" or whatever command you would like to use for this trick, open your fist and give your dog the treat. Repeat this process three times and then take a

Lots of fun can be
had simply with a stick
discovered on a walk!

break. Your blind dog will learn this trick in next to no time!

• PUTTING HIS FRONT PAWS ON A CHAIR

You can easily teach your blind dog how to place his front legs on an armchair. It can be another item of furniture, of course, such as an upturned washing basket, but take care in this case that the basket doesn't slip as this would give your dog a fright and undermine his enthusiasm.

Place the armchair/basket in front of the dog (tell him what you are doing so that he doesn't become anxious). When your dog sniffs the chair, praise him and give him a treat. Do this a couple of times and he will realise that he is supposed to do something with the chair. As soon as he touches the chair with his paw, reward him and show him you are pleased by praising him. Acknowledge this particular behaviour until he has understood what it is that he is really meant to be doing, then you can introduce a signal word (eg "Touch").

Don't worry that your dog will constantly be up on the furniture just because he knows this trick.

• OPENING A DRAWER

Learning and demonstrating tricks gives dogs pride in themselves. You can show your blind dog how to open a drawer, and he will definitely enjoy helping you around the house.

Tie a soft cord to the drawer handle. The aim is to get your dog to open the drawer by pulling on the cord when you give the command.

Hold the cord to your blind dog's muzzle until he begins to take an interest in it, at which point, praise him and reward with a treat. As soon as he takes the cord in his mouth, progress to rewarding for this behaviour only. Always try to praise your dog exactly at the moment that he demonstrates the behaviour for which you are aiming. This means paying very close attention and being very quick with the praise.

If your dog begins to pull on the cord, reward him at once, even if the drawer doesn't open (because he's not pulling hard enough or is not standing right in front of it), as that isn't important at this stage.

Progress very slowly to avoid frustrating your dog and finish the exercises as soon as he does the trick. It is important that both you and your dog enjoy yourselves and feel a sense of achievement.

When your dog has understood what he is supposed to do, introduce the signal word, for example "Drawer out." Subsequently, you can teach him to shut the drawer by saying "Drawer in."

Be creative and you will certainly be able to think up plenty of fun games for your blind dog!

Catch!

Chapter 10

Smellorama! scent work

Scent work is a meaningful and species-appropriate way of occupying your dog.

Laying simple, short scent trails
Everything that moves or is moved across the ground leaves a scent trail: people, for example, or animals, but also insects and even vehicles. This is because the ground is disturbed, which results in odours. The scent is at its strongest after about fifteen minutes and begins to fade after about one-and-a-half to two hours. Scent strength is affected by the age of the trail, the weather (damp, cold ground makes it easier for dogs to follow the trail), and the type of terrain: soft soil has more of a smell than sand, for instance, and a trail on frozen ground will fade very slowly.

In order to do scent work, you need a chest harness for your dog, a 5-10 metre lead, and tasty treats that your dog likes.

To begin with, your dog has to learn to follow one short trail: when she is on the trail, reward her by carrying on; if she leaves the trail, stop.

Ask someone to help you by holding your dog whilst you lay the trail (if your dog is particularly anxious or timid, it is perhaps better for you to hold your dog and ask your helper to lay the trail). Keep the first trail fairly short: between 30 and 50cm.

Lay the first trail on soft ground; simple, safe terrain for your blind dog, preferably a field. Mark your starting point so that you don't forget where it is. Place a reward at the end of the scent trail – for example, some meat – then carry straight on and leave the area of the scent trail.

Collect your dog and take her to the start of the trail. If she leaves the trail, stand still and, when she returns to the trail, reward her by continuing.

You can also lay a drag trail for your first trail: the scent that you drag behind you increases the

Elliott enthusiastically follows a scent.

Tüddel goes through the beer mats and indicates the right one – which has the scent – by lying down in front of it.

dog's motivation, and she will quickly associate the trail scent with finding the food. At the end of the trail, the dog always gets what has been dragged to make the trail. Gradually reduce the use of the drag scent.

Off-lead locate and retrieve

The objective here is for your dog to learn to search for something specific within a designated area.

Initially, this should be a small area as the larger the area, the higher the dog's stress level. Begin by using an object that your dog likes, such as a rag toy or a Kong™. Before you start, consider whether or not your dog likes to retrieve items. If this is not the case, she should just indicate where the item is.

The off-lead locate and retrieve course is created using a scent trail. Place two small markers in a field about ten metres apart and walk a zigzag course between them, dropping the toy somewhere in the middle of the course. Take your dog to the beginning of the scent trail. She should be able to pick out the search area for herself, but if she goes significantly off-course, call her back. In general, however, it is better not to try to influence what she is doing as this can unsettle and distract her.

After a few successful attempts, you can introduce a command, and later extend the size of the working area. Make sure to put the toy in a variety of different places: much later, when your dog knows exactly what she is doing, you can dispense with the scent trail. When you get to this stage, initially place the toy in the first place that your dog is likely to search. Later, you will be able to simply throw it and use the command to send your dog to find it.

Laying a scent trail.

For more on scent work, see Smellorama! Nose games for dogs (Veloce Publishing)

Case history
WINNIE

Winnie - a golden cocker spaniel - met up with her owner, Niki, in Vejer de la Frontera, south-west Spain, where Niki had recently moved. Niki's friends, Lesley and Derek, regularly took in and rehoused stray dogs, and asked Niki if she would take Winnie; that night Winnie had a bath and slept at the foot of Niki's bed!

Winnie was incredibly docile and quiet, and would accompany Niki to the office, sleeping under the desk all day; in fact, wherever Niki went, so did Winnie.

Niki's vet estimated that Winnie was 6 or 7 years old, yet she was very active and loved going to the beach, where she would chase kites and seagulls for hours on end. Not only did she enjoy chasing kites but also shadows; the reflection of a watch or a CD on the garden wall would get her so excited that she would be transfixed for hours.

Niki feels that Winnie went blind very suddenly, although earlier signs that she noticed - such as sleeping more, not being able to identify Niki on the beach, and going in the wrong direction when called - could indicate that Winnie was having problems prior to this.

Niki noticed that Winnie's eyes were becoming bluey-coloured and clouded; initially the left eye and literally overnight. The vet confirmed Winnie was blind in one eye due to cataracts, although could still see perfectly out of the right eye. However, within a few months this eye had also become discoloured and she was finding it difficult to negotiate her way around, bumping into doors and chairs in the night en route to the kitchen for a drink of water.

A visit to the vet to enquire about a cataract operation was disheartening as he felt that Winnie was perhaps too old to make it viable.

Despite her blindness Winnie is a very happy dog. During the day she has a wander round the garden, using the walls of the villa to guide herself. She can climb stairs quite easily but will not come down them unless someone is right next to her to coax her down. She is absolutely fine with people and loves company, but other dogs annoy her and she sulks if there is one about. She does still love to travel in the car, so if Niki goes out for a short drive she will sit in the footwell.

Niki is careful about where she places furniture, and where bikes and plant pots are left as Winnie knows her routes around the house and garden, and any new or moved object becomes a hazard. The vet advised that her bed and food/water bowls remain in the same place so that she always knows where to find them. Winnie loves to sit underneath things, enjoying the feeling of security that this gives. Her favourite spots indoors are under the bed or under the table, and outside in the garden she will crawl underneath the sun loungers.

Niki and husband Joaquin are very careful to talk to Winnie to let her know when they are nearby so that she isn't startled; walking into a room where Winnie is, Niki will whistle or make a clicking noise so she knows that someone is there.

Winnie has lubricating drops in her eyes, which she finds soothing, and enjoys it when Niki massages the eye area.

Because Niki returns to the UK fairly frequently, she has to make special arrangements for Winnie's care, as she is not happy to leave her in kennels. Winnie usually remains in her own home and friends or neighbours visit to feed and check on her.

Twice a year Winnie goes to be professionally clipped, and is said to be the salon's most well behaved and noble client! Niki says that Winnie does not complain about anything; the only time she does whine is when she can smell bacon and sausages cooking. In this instance, it could be said that her blindness works in her favour as everyone feels sorry for her and gives her food, which probably wouldn't happen quite so often if she could see!

On Niki's wedding day, when Winnie still had her sight.

Chapter 11

Training tips

Of course, there is no secret recipe for how to train a blind dog, because every dog is different. However, it does help to remember a few specific points when dealing with a blind dog:

● First, keep your dog on a lead (3-5 metre length) and allow him to investigate the training area and any obstacles, such as any apparatus, so that he doesn't later bump into them. Let him go around the area several times, as this will help him to feel safe. Most blind dogs feel unsettled when they are in unfamiliar surroundings – some more so than others – so it is therefore particularly important that he gains a positive first impression of the situation and the surroundings.

It is essential that he becomes familiar with the training area.

● Make a point of organising your training sessions so that you always have the first few in the same place.

● Don't take your dog off the lead until you feel that he knows and is comfortable in the new environment.

● Talk to your dog even more than you would a sighted dog.

● Many blind dogs don't like being touched by strangers and have a hypersensitive reaction to being touched.

● When you call your dog, repeat the call several times so that he can locate you.

● Many blind dogs experience problems walking on unfamiliar surfaces: watch out for this.

● Don't forget that blind dogs have only limited opportunities for communication. They can't read calming signals, and, of course, are unable to see gestures or facial expressions.

● Keep in mind that blind dogs assess risks differently to sighted dogs, and in extreme cases can't assess them at all. They react best to neutral things: over-friendly, excitable people can seem threatening, as blind dogs have no way of properly assessing the situation. This makes it all the more important to prepare him for situations such as being put on the lead and being approached by other people.

● Don't use a pole or anything similar to guide your dog. Doing this must be really awful for the animal, as he is then even more limited in how he can express himself.

● Teach signal words that allow your dog to know what is going to happen next.

Don't take your dog off the lead straight away.

Chapter 12

Conclusion

Anyone who advises you to have your blind dog put down, simply doesn't know any better. We humans tend to live in our own subjective reality, and pass judgement on things that we don't know or understand, and can't relate to. We are very quick to pigeonhole people and their deeds and lives as 'different,' and it's not easy to recategorise them. In fact, we sometimes have a hard time seeing past the end of our own nose.

At moments like this, when we are tempted to judge, we should take a deep breath and try to see things from a different perspective.

Just recently, I was out walking with Trolli the blind dog and his owner, and watching him run across the fields; his obvious delight in doing so said more than any book ever could.

I hope that my book will help you and your dog have regard for each other in everyday life, and enjoy your time together. Also that you have found some tips and information that will help you with training.

Never forget the blind dog's basic requirement for mutual trust and respect: you are your dog's eyes. You must see for her and guide her safely through her life. When she speaks to you, listen carefully and respond to her. Have patience with your dog and with yourself in every situation.

Rogues' Gallery

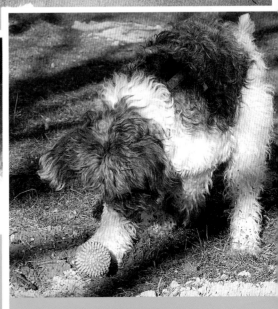

Further reading

Smellorama! Nose games for dogs
Viviane Theby. Hubble and Hattie, Veloce Publishing Ltd

Know Your Dog: The guide to a beautiful relationship
Immanuel Birmelin. Hubble and Hattie, Veloce Publishing Ltd

Dog Tricks: Fun and games for your clever canine
Mary Ray and Justine Harding. Kynos Verlag

The Guide Dog's Book of Ultimate Dog Care
Sue Guthrie, Dick Lane and G Sumner-Smith. Ringpress Books

The Complete Massage Manual: Gentle Dog Care
Julia Robertson. Hubble and Hattie, Veloce Publishing Ltd

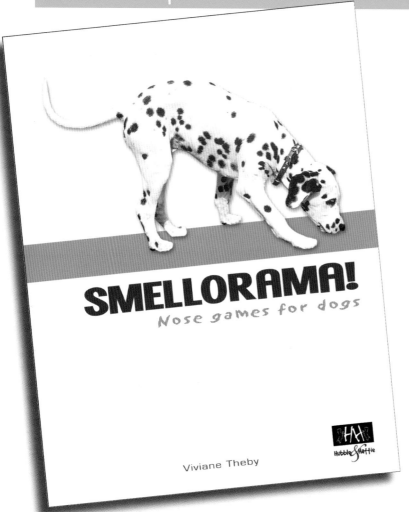

SMELLORAMA!
Nose games for dogs

Viviane Theby

How does your dog smell? Very well, as it happens!

★ How a dog's nose functions ★ What your dog is telling you
★ Scent discrimination ★ Sit, stand, down ★ Hide and seek
★ Laying a track ★ Changing scents ★ Retrieving
★ Searching for people ★ City training ★ Enrich your dog's life
and your understanding of a dog's world

Paperback with flaps. 80 pages. 220mm tall x 170mm. 37 colour pictures/37 mono drawings. ISBN 978-1-845842-93-2/UPC 6-36847-04293-6. £9.99 UK/$19.95 USA

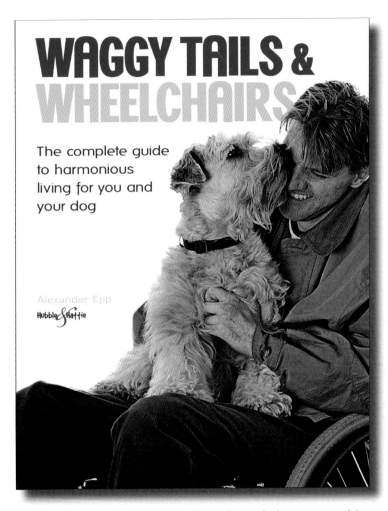

WAGGY TAILS & WHEELCHAIRS

The complete guide to harmonious living for you and your dog

Alexander Epp

Hubble & Hattie

★ A wheelchair is no barrier to dog ownership! ★ Benefits of dog ownership ★ Positive effects on state of mind ★ Basic considerations ★ Physical restrictions ★ Caring for your dog ★ Walkin' the dog ★ Clothing ★ Special equipment ★ Suitable breeds ★ Dog size and temperament ★ Ability/selection/acquisition ★ Training for a special life ★ Walking behaviour ★ Nighttime excursions ★ Winter-time ★ The law, you and your dog ★ On tour ★ Wheelchair, dog and competition ★ Water sport ★ Your dog and travelling ★ Ideas for trips ★ Wheelchair, dog and traffic ★ General problems ★ Where next? ★ Appendix

Paperback with flaps. 96 pages. 220mm tall x 170mm. 18 colour pictures, 9 mono. ISBN 978-1-845842-92-5/UPC 6-36847-04292-9 £12.99 UK/$24.95 USA

For more info on Hubble and Hattie titles, visit our website at www.hubbleandhattie.com
email: info@hubbleandhattie.com • tel: 44 (0)1305 260068 • prices subject to change • p&p extra

More from Hubble and Hattie

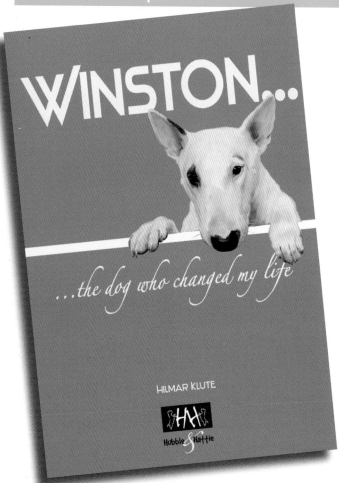

WINSTON...

...the dog who changed my life

HILMAR KLUTE

Hubble & Hattie

★ Winston was a puppy, found abandoned and tethered to a gravestone in a city cemetery ★ The true story of how a non-dog lover unexpectedly became a dog owner ★ Experience the strange, new and unfamiliar world of dogs and their owners from a complete newcomer's perspective ★ A charming and irreverent story ★ Reveals some surprising truths about the relationship between dog and man ★ Casts a critical eye over the professional 'dog whisperer' ★ Will appeal to many kinds of reader: those who know nothing about dogs, those who love dogs, and perhaps even those who cannot stand dogs!

Hardback & jacket. 160 pages. 180mm tall x 120mm. Drawings throughout. ISBN 978-1-845842-74-1/UPC 6-36847-04274-5. £9.99 UK/$17.95 USA

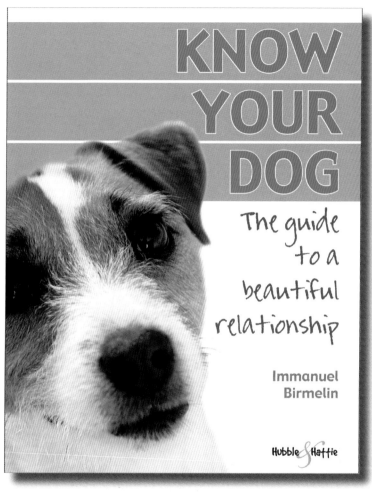

Recognise your dog's personality ★ A world of emotions ★ Emotions can be guided ★ A dog's senses ★ How dogs learn and reason ★ Playful training ★ How does a dog see itself? ★ Recognising skills and helping them develop ★ Sleeping and dreaming ★ The daily mental workout ★ Learning exercises with 'zing' ★ Exercises to keep your dog fit ★ Tricky tests of logic ★ Memory training ★ Tips and information

Hardback. 96 pages. 220mm tall x 165mm. 76 colour pictures.
ISBN 978-1-845840-72-3/UPC 6-36847-04072-7 £9.99

For more info on Hubble and Hattie titles, visit our website at www.hubbleandhattie.com
email: info@hubbleandhattie.com • tel: 44 (0)1305 260068 • prices subject to change • p&p extra

Important notes